THE GREEN LINDEN

The
GREEN LINDEN

Selected Lithuanian Folksongs

Edited by
ALGIRDAS LANDSBERGIS
and CLARK MILLS

With a Foreword by ROBERT PAYNE

an Introduction by MARIJA GIMBUTAS

and illustrations by VIKTORAS PETRAVIČIUS

VOYAGES PRESS
New York

THE GREEN LINDEN
Copyright © 1964, by
VOYAGES PRESS

First edition, 1964

Library of Congress Catalog Card No. 64-7658

VOYAGES PRESS
35 WEST 75TH STREET
NEW YORK 23, N. Y.

PRINTED IN THE UNITED STATES OF AMERICA BY
Theo. Gaus' Sons, Inc., Brooklyn 1, N. Y.

TABLE OF CONTENTS

V. MARRIAGE

VI. FAMILY LIFE

VII. ORPHANS

VIII. WORK

IX. WAR

X. LAMENTS

Foreword: On the Dainos

It sometimes happens that when the snows melt on the mountains, there can be found high up mysterious snowfields which never melt, however strongly the sun beats down on them. These snowfields scattered about the summits remain through all seasons: the centuries pass, and they are always there. So it is with cultures: here and there we come upon patches of brightness which linger on against all expectation and seemingly against all reason. Some prodigious power of survival breathes through them. We tell ourselves that they should have perished long ago, but they haunt us with their immortality.

The *dainos* of Lithuania are like those snowfields. They seem to have been sung from time immemorial, and they are still being sung. They owe their survival to their poetic power, and also to the very nature of the country which gave them birth, a country hemmed in by forests, swamps and seas, outside the main highways of European civilization. They represent a form of poetry as ancient as anything on this earth, for they are essentially spells, incantations, offerings to the gods. Though they are simple and immediately comprehensible, they do not belong to the world we know. There is about them something steady and direct like the eyes of animals. These poems to the gods show no fear, nor do they plead for mercy.

These poems are never oblique; there are no *arrière-pensées*, no efforts to embroider outside the naked lyrical thrust; the songs sing themselves, and they ask only that they should be permitted to sing. One comes to them almost unbelieving, surprised that such perfect songs should be permitted to survive. They have a beauty and pure primitive splendor above anything I know in Western literature except the early songs of the Greek islanders. They seem to have been written at the morning of the world, and the dew is still on them.

7

The people who wrote and sang them are among the most enviable who ever lived. They had a deep instinctive feeling for the simplest of all things—for woods and running water and girls' faces and the colors of the sky. They sang artlessly, but how much art there is in their artlessness! They sang with the full voice, conscious of their power to summon the gods at their bidding, conscious of their pride, their mortal splendor. For them the world is washed clean by the heavenly rains, and neither guilt nor regret have worked on them.

We are accustomed to believe that great poetry springs out of great and powerful civilizations; and we point to Hellas and the Spain of the Conquistadors and Elizabethan England—these countries were so powerful that they shook the world, and something of their power entered their poetry. But poetry does not necessarily, or even very often, spring from imperial power, of which there was little enough in Weimar, and there must have been even less in the courts of the troubadour princes of southern France. Poetry comes to birth whenever men come to their maturity. It is a thing of the innocent eye and the innocent tongue, and of the wayward human spirit which manifests itself in obscure places. We do not know why the first Greek songs were sung on an obscure island of the Aegean, but they were; nor do we know why there was such a proliferation of song in Lithuania, so obscure a country that the histories of Europe pass it by in silence or with a brief mention of the Teutonic knights. But Lithuania, too, has its imperial tradition, as the Russians learned to their cost. Of that imperial tradition there is no sign in the *dainos*.

To set the *dainos* in their proper context we must look back, I believe, to the earliest surviving songs from China in the collection called *The Book of Poetry*, which may have been compiled by Confucius. Here, for example, are two songs, one Chinese, the other Lithuanian:

> *Heiho, the sun in the east!*
> *This lovely man*
> *Enters my chamber,*
> *Enters my chamber,*
> *And steps through my door.*

8

Heiho, the sun in the east!
This lovely man
Enters my garden,
Enters my garden,
And steps over the threshold.

＊　　＊　　＊　　＊

O little sun, God's daughter,
Where have you been dwelling?
Where have you been straying?
Why have you left us alone?

—I have kept shepherds warm,
I have shielded the orphans
Beyond the seas and mountains.

O little sun, God's daughter,
Who kindled the fires in the evening?
Who kindled the fires in the evening?
Who made your bed for you?

O morning and evening star!
The morning star my fire,
The evening star my bed.
Many kinsmen have blessed me,
And many are my treasures.

It is not only, of course, that the Chinese poem has similarities of form with the Lithuanian poem, and they share the same crisp, sensuous quality, but they speak of the sun with an exquisite friendliness and enjoyment, without ceremony. The sun and the poet speak to one another in terms of intimacy, enchanted with one another's presence. There are sexual overtones: in one poem the sun is masculine, in the other feminine, but essentially both poets are speaking of the same sun, *because there is no other and it is unthinkable that there should be any other.* They see the sun which is created anew every morning, the everlasting day eternally revived for the pleasure and delight of those who bask in its splendor.

In our own age such simple joys are rare, and we are in danger of forgetting that there was a time when joy existed on the earth, when men could say: "Many kinsmen have blessed me, and many

9

are my treasures." Our sun is an atomic pile menacing us with deadly radiations. Theirs was a face which peered down at them every morning and went away for a little while each night. So it is throughout the *dainos*: the world of nature shines with kindly face and with a quiet delight in human preoccupations. Man, far from being alienated, far from being mysteriously cut off from the sources of power, is the friend and lover of all creation.

This is why, in our desperate age, the *dainos* acquire a supreme importance, for they speak of a time when joy still walked over the earth.

ROBERT PAYNE

Introduction: The Antiquity of the Daina

In 1940 I went to Dzūkija, a sandy, hilly land in southeastern Lithuania, to write down the texts of *dainos* sung by an old woman from her repertory of more than 300 songs. In almost every corner of Lithuania could be found women reputed to be "great singers." They were the last bards of Lithuania, the chief transmitters of its heritage from past ages to the 20th century, and the last vestiges of an era which is fast disintegrating today. From the gifts of these women the Lithuanian folkloristic archives have filled their dower chests during the past two centuries. The archives of the Academy of Sciences in Vilnius now boast more than 200,000 texts of *dainos* and about 30,000 melodies. Some thousands of these have been collected in many volumes. (See Bibliography, page 133.)

The woman, reaping oats with a sickle, sang in full voice. This was "a sacrifice to the gods" in the best meaning of the phrase—a personal, and collectively sanctioned, need. Even by the best singers in the world, the *daina* cannot be performed on a stage with equal feeling and power, because it cannot be separated from its environment. As the woman sang, the earth seemed to move and breathe hope, together with the *daina's* three-tone melody and simple rhythm.

* * *

In the *daina*, melody and words were created at the same moment, as a song; taken separately, the two elements lose much of their value. We search in vain for a fixed prosody in the verses; the words were adjusted to the melody, to special rhythms: to reaping, to plucking, to swinging, to weaving, to the flight of a bird, to a wedding dance, to a game. Hence the continual repetition of phrases, the abundant use of refrains and little words that appear only in songs, such as *lylia, lylia; lingo rito ta ta to;* or

11

dobile dobilėli ("clover, little clover"). Some of these little words, while they have no separate meaning, suggest the rhythms and sounds of work. A few work *dainos* are known that consist only of such refrains:

> *Saduto, tuto!*
> *Saduto, tuto!*
> *Sadu, sadu, tuto,*
> *Saduto, tuto!*
> *Tuto, saduto!*
> *Tuto, saduto!*

The *dainos* are remarkable for their almost infinite number of diminutives, which often create the effect of rhyme. They lend to the *daina* its characteristic softness and tenderness of sound of expression. Among the diminutives most commonly used are: *motinėle* ("little mother"); *saulelė* ("little sun"); *mergužėlė* ("little maiden"); *baltoji lelijėlė* ("little white lily"); *bernužėlis* ("little lad"); and *baltasis dobilėlis* ("little white clover").

The syllable *ėl* (pronounced ăl) embellishes the language of the *dainos*, which is otherwise overladen with s, š, z, and ž sounds.

It has been said that *brolis* ("brother") can be expressed 300 different ways in the diminutive in Lithuanian. Countless diminutives can be derived from such words as *motina* ("mother"), *sesuo* ("sister"), *tėvas* ("father"), *liepa* ("linden"), and others. Sometimes more than half the words in a stanza are diminutives.

* * *

The *daina* is manifold and many-layered. Some layers are old, some are recent, and some contain ancient elements fused with others from later historic periods. The *daina* was transmitted orally from generation to generation and was continually altered. Thus not one *daina* with a firmly established text exists. Even the same person, on different days, may sing the same *daina* in somewhat different ways. Certain *dainos* in published collections have several variations. The elements most strongly fixed in Lithuanian songs are their mythological images, and others related to an archaic, patriarchal family life and to agricultural work.

In this collection, *dainos* are classified under ten headings:

mythology, nature, love and courtship, singing and drinking, marriage, family life, orphans, work, war, and laments. The contents make up the peasant's life, his observation of nature, his participation in the rotation of the seasons, his dependence on the blessed life-bringing natural forces and on the constantly threatening powers of evil and death. Much was sung of love and courtship, marriage, and the destiny of a married woman. This inevitable cycle of human life is portrayed in the *dainos* as an intense drama, which begins with a young maiden thriving in her father's and mother's house, "the white lily" whose youth and innocence are compared to the green rue (the wreath of rue is the symbol of chastity); continues with her dreams and expectation of meeting a lad, "the white clover," coming on a bay steed; culminates in the wedding ceremony and the painful departure of the bride from her beloved mother, father, sisters, and brothers; and ends with her unhappy life in an alien house, suffering from a mother-in-law and not infrequently from an unkind husband. A tone of resignation and fatalism replaces the mood of joyful days and the mother's tender love. An unhappy life may be foreseen even in her father's house:

> O wreath of rue that crowns my head,
> how long shall you stay green and glad?

A picture of maidenly joy and conjugal sadness is dramatically drawn in these lines:

> The wreath was sung over.
> The veil was sighed over.

The tragedy comes from the strict patriarchal rule: the girl has no free will to marry; she weds a boy of her father's choice, not a true love of her own. Echoes of stealing or buying a bride can still be found in the folklore. Another ancient feature, going back to the Indo-European common homeland, is horsemanship and an unusual love for horses. On horseback the lad comes to visit his maiden; on horseback the farmers and warriors and kings of early Lithuanian history rode to the world of the dead. The steed (*žirgas*) and not the work horse (*arklys*) appears in the songs. A fast bay steed is the dream and pride of youth. In the

13

dainos even a simple village lad rides a gold-shod bay, with a silver bridle and gold-embroidered saddle—an indication of the importance of the horse and a reminiscence of the well-harnessed companion of warriors in days long past.

* * *

The *dainos* are predominantly lyrical; epic elements are few, being found in only a limited number of ballads. It seems that the Lithuanian *epos* slowly disappeared with the end of the imperial period of Lithuania, perhaps in about the 16th century. We can only surmise its existence from the many legends about acropolises, sunken castles, treasure hoards and their royal masters, and from a few songs that mention names of kings and warriors. The legends are petrified remnants of a remote past. The Lithuanian nobility was largely Slavonized between the 17th and 19th centuries. The *daina* was abandoned by the courts, but it lived on in the villages, faithfully preserved by the poorest people of the country, guarded by the mother of the family, during the darkest period of Lithuanian history: the occupation by tsarist Russia between 1795 and 1918.

The history of the past two centuries molded the final shape of the *dainos*. Much that concerned the life of the upper classes was no doubt lost, especially since the *dainos* were not written down before the 18th century. Yet the shelter of the thatched roof did preserve a unique treasure: the *daina*'s profound antiquity, simplicity, and subtlety, unspoiled by the world we know.

* * *

The Lithuanians are Indo-Europeans; together with the Latvians, they make up the Baltic group. They speak one of the most archaic living Indo-European tongues, one closely related to the *satem* groups, even the Sanskrit of the Vedic hymns. The same close relations, and the archaism, are observed in the mythology.

It is not at all astonishing that we find some parallelism between the Lithuanian *dainos* and the earliest surviving songs from China, as Robert Payne has indicated in the Foreword, or that Lithuanian words are comparable with Sanskrit words recorded 3,000 years ago. The ancestors of all the Indo-European speakers in Europe

14

came from the Eurasian prairies sometime earlier than 2,000 B.C. (as many archaeologists, ethnologists, and linguists, as well as the present author, tend to believe). Thus their perception of nature and their concept of gods have Oriental correlates. Hence the similarity of Lithuanian mythology to the ancient Indic, Persian, Greek, Thracian, Old Germanic, Italic, and Celtic.

*   *   *

The question naturally arises, why the Lithuanian language, mythology, and *daina* are replete with elements belonging to "the morning of the world," which many other nations of the Indo-European family have long since lost. The answer seems to lie in the geographic and historic destiny of Lithuania. The Balts settled in the forested zone of northeastern Europe. In the Bronze and Iron ages their territories covered a large area from the Baltic Sea to present-day central Russia—as archaeological finds and Baltic names for rivers indicate.

The Lithuanian language, together with the Lettish, belongs to the eastern Baltic group, and the Lithuanians, in the very center, were ringed by other Baltic-speaking tribes. For millennia the ancestors of the Lithuanians were shielded from strong outside influences. Their homes were not on the crossroads of migration of the Scythians, Celts, and Germanic tribes. Thinly settled in the great expanses of a forested land with many rivers, lakes, and swamps full of animals, fish, and birds, mushrooms, nuts, honey, and berries, they felt no need to seek better land or pastures, as did the Goths and other Germanic tribes, or the Celts and the semi-nomadic Scythians.

Their ties with Mother Earth were strengthened even more with the gradual progress of agriculture during the last two millennia, as river-valley regions were cleared and turned into arable land. The rich natural environment absorbed the Lithuanian soul, sustaining in it a profound veneration for the living land with its deciduous and coniferous trees and wildflowers, and an intimate relation with the animal world. The Lithuanians and their kin tribes did not lose their ability to see nature intensely: their vision, for all the creatures of the earth, was as acute as a hawk's. Hence the multitude of parallelisms of human life with that of nature in the *dainos*. Hence, too, the onomatopoeiac sounds which imi-

15

tate the trill of the nightingale, the call of the swallow, the hum of the bee; the rustling of forests, or rye fields, or the wind.

The Lithuanians were among the last of the Indo-European groups of Europe to which Christianity was introduced. Although Lithuania was officially Christianized in 1387, the villagers retained the old religion for many more centuries, since clergymen could not understand the native language and since Latin was meaningless to their rural parishioners. More success in converting the Lithuanians to Christianity was achieved during the Reformation and Counter-Reformation in the 16th century, when the first catechisms appeared in Lithuanian; yet even then, and almost, until the 20th century, ancient beliefs and customs persisted. The popular religion slowly developed into a "double faith," as Lithuanian folklore maintained its pagan foundations and remained faithful to its roots deep in prehistory. Hence the many mythological elements in the *dainos*. Lithuanian and Latvian folklore, alone in Europe, can boast a living ancient mythology with a number of names of pagan gods and other mythological images, comparable to pre-Olympian Greek, Roman, Vedic Indian, Persian, and Old Scandinavian. Even the ancient Slavic gods are less well preserved; their names were replaced relatively early by those of Christian saints.

The Green Linden, like other collections, opens with mythological songs—rare and precious jewels. In content these represent the oldest layer of the *dainos*. But do we really understand the symbolic language, in which *Dievas* ("God"), "*Dievas*' steeds," *Saulė* ("Sun"), often known as "God's daughter," *Aušrinė* ("Morning Star"), *Vakarinė* ("Evening Star"), *Perkūnas* ("the Thunderer"), *oželis* ("the little he-goat"), the oak, the linden, and other trees, animals, and birds play their parts? Not infrequently these are represented simply as poetic devices. To many researchers the *daina* has the quality of a prolonged dream, not to be profaned by reality. Is this not because it is a part of the ancient world in which our ancestors lived? I wish therefore to touch on at least some elements of the mythology, or "image of the world," in which the ancestors of present-day Lithuanians believed, collectively and emotionally. Without the insights afforded by mythology, we could not uncover the basic traits of the *dainos*, just as we could never learn fully to appreciate ancient

16

Greek poetry, vase paintings, and sculptures without an acquaintance with Greek mythology.

* * *

Baltic mythology, as it can be reconstructed from folklore and, medieval historical sources, is Indo-European *par excellence*. The gods' images reflect the old Indo-European social structure with its three basic classes: the ruling, the warrior, and the agricultural. Since, however, the mythological elements were transmitted by peasants alone, only the divine figures connected with the farmer's mentality lived on in the folklore: those which influence plant, animal, and human life, which fructify the life-giving earth, which fend off by purification the perpetually threatening evil powers. For this reason the sun, the moon, and *Perkūnas* are most often, encountered in folk belief, song, and incantation.

The word "God" used in translations should not be confused with the Christian God. The Baltic *Dievas* is an analogue of the Germanic *Tiu* (*Tyr*) and of the Indic *Mitra*. He is the guardian and stimulator of crops, and is inseparable from his divine horses (*Dievo žirgai*—"God's steeds") in silver harnesses with golden saddles and stirrups. His farmstead lies beyond the sky; beyond the stone, silver, gold, or amber hill. From this hill *Dievas* rides, on horseback or in a chariot of gold or copper, holding golden reins with golden tassels. He approaches the earth slowly and extremely carefully, lest he shake off the dewdrops and snowball-tree blossoms, lest he halt the growth of shoots or hinder the work of sower and ploughman. He raises up the rye, he steps on weed grass.

Dievas (pronounced 'dẽ-e-väs) was god of the shining sky; like the Vedic *Devas*, he was a superior god on whose account the sun and moon and the day are bright. His appearance was that of a Baltic king. In Latvian *dainos* he is represented as a most handsome man, dressed in a silver gown and cap, with a sword at his belt. He had twin sons, *Dievo sūneliai*, "the riders," inseparable from *Dievas*' steeds.

In the pantheon, *Dievas*' closest relations were with *Laima*, the goddess of fate, who also decreed the "sun's day" and foretold the happiness and unhappiness in human lives, and their length. Her name is connected with *laimé* ("happiness") and with the

17

verb *leisti* ("to create"). "So *Laima* has allotted" is a frequent expression in songs.

Saulė ("the Sun") was a separate divinity analogous to the Greek *Helios* and the Indic *Savits*. "O little Sun, God's daughter" —this epithet is almost certainly not an expression of an emotional attitude toward the sun, but derives from the ancient hierarchy of the pantheon. The moon, likewise, was subsidiary. A "prince" rather than a ruler, he was called *Dievaitis* (diminutive of *Dievas*).

"God's daughter" is a dominant figure in mythological songs, and a personalized one. Unlike the arrangement in almost all other mythologies, the Baltic sun is feminine while the moon is masculine. The moon weds the sun. She is the mother, the moon is the father. "Sun mother, you, sun mother, gather a dowry. . . ." Her femininity and motherly qualities are a special Baltic trait, a concept whose age cannot be traced. Other features of the sun-goddess go deep into antiquity. Prayers to *Saulė*, as to a goddess, must be said with one's head uncovered:

> The father was walking
> By the edge of the field,
> By the edge of the rye-field.
> He entreated the sun
> Without a hat, without a fur cap. . . .

Veneration of the sun reached its peak at summer solstice, on the morning of June 24. At dawn the sun dances on a silver hill, changes colors, plays, hops, jumps like a lamb. Everyone, young and old, rises early to see the sun's triumph. She also sails in a golden boat:

> He lied who said that
> *Saulė* travels afoot:
> Over the forest, she rides in a chariot;
> Over the sea, she sails in a boat.*

At winter solstice the Lithuanians celebrated the sun's returning. In Christmas songs, *Kalėda* (the present word for Christmas, joined with the Latin *calendae*) is the sun, holding silken whips as she comes over high hills and low valleys on iron wheels, or

* Latvian *daina*.

appears as a nine-horned stag. One song (see page 35) is replete with ancient symbolic images: the nine-horned stag and the smiths hammering and forging a golden cup. What is this golden cup? Again it is the sun, since the sun was also seen as a fluid substance, bringing blessings to plant life and beauty to maidens' faces. The smiths recall the Heavenly Smith, *Kalvis*, the Baltic *Hephaestus*, who in old days hammered a sun for the god of celestial light. He hammered a ring or crown for the Morning Star and a silver belt and golden stirrups for *Dievas*' sons, as we know from Latvian *dainos*.

When *Kalvis* hammers, silver pieces fall down from the heavens to the Daugava River. His hammer is gigantic—with it he struggles against countless obstructions and frees the sun from imprisonment, as Lithuanians still believed in the 15th century. *Kalvis* (or *Kalvelis* in the diminutive), was a warrior-god like the Indic *Indra Vrtrahan*, a dragon-killing hero. Even his name is connected with the verb *kauti* ("to slay") and *kova* ("the battle").

Another warrior-god, who appears often in the *dainos* and whose image is one of the liveliest in Baltic folklore, is *Perkūnas*, god of thunder and lightning, rain-shedder and overseer of right and order. His name has the same origin as the verb *per-ti* ("to strike"). He smites evil people, liars, thieves, and selfish or vain persons. He does not tolerate the moon's infidelity, and cleaves him with a sword (see page 27). The Lithuanians say, "May the dear god *Perkūnas* smite you because of your lying." He tosses his lightning-bolts or axes like the Greek *Zeus-Keraunos*, Germanic *Thor*, Slavic *Perun*, and other thunder-gods of the Indo-European mythology.

An even more important function of *Perkūnas* was to purify and fructify the Mother Earth. The first thunder in the spring shakes the earth; the grass begins to grow quickly, grains take root, trees turn green. Earth lies barren until Thunder smites her, until this sky-god weds her. Like *Zeus*, he bedews the earth and makes it moist. Dew is the divine seed; in the *dainos* it is golden or silver: "Droplets of dew shine like silver buds." *Perkūnas*' sacred tree is the oak, and he himself scatters heavenly seeds so that oaks can grow. The seeds are carried by birds, usually by gray doves.

In the *dainos* and in folk art there is a symbolic life-tree with

19

glittering cones or buds: "In every branchlet a golden bud, on the toplet the cuckoo leans." These buds shine in gold, silver, pearl, and diamond—colors of the shining sky and its divinities. They are as mysterious and sacred as the mistletoe. The cuckoo (the prophet of human life) or dove or woodpecker on the toplet is the transmitter of Perkūnas' mana to earth. These birds perch at the top of a nine-branched spruce or linden, just as in symbolic portrayals by the Mycenaean Greeks and Cretans of almost 3,000 years ago they perch on a tree or an obelisk.

The numerous epithets used in dainos—golden apples, pearl leaves, silver streams—seem to draw us into fairy worlds. Actually, they lead into the early mythological image—the concept that there is divinity where Earth and Heaven meet. This mythological motif in the Lithuanian daina, however modified and freely applied, is usually of intense beauty, as in the version of the daina which begins, "Hey, nowhere, nowhere. . . ." (see page 47).

In the animal world Perkūnas also has his representatives; the he-goat and the bull. They are endowed with this God's powers: fructification and weather prophecy. The he-goat (ožys, or diminutive, oželis) is often encountered in songs and dances. A well-known daina begins with the words: "The little he-goat jumped into a rue garden. What will happen, dear Mother, what will happen?" As an incarnation of Perkūnas' mana, the he-goat was the main sacrificial animal. One remarkable daina (see page 29) still recalls the sacrifice by priests of a he-goat on a cliff by the river.

On the cliff by the river, says the same daina, "a fire burns day and night." High on a hill the sacred tribal fire was guarded by priests. Once a year, on the eve of the midsummer festival, it was symbolically extinguished, then kindled again. The Lithuanians held fire sacred and called it eternal, according to Eneo Silvio, writing at the beginning of the 15th century. A sacred fire, as purifying element and symbol of happiness, was also kept in each house until the 20th century, carefully guarded by the mother of the family.

Many birds appear in the dainos. The cuckoo, the dove, and the woodpecker belong to the divine sphere of Perkūnas. White birds, such as the swan with its mysterious long neck, are associated with the sun-god. One bird, the falcon Sakalas, with invul-

20

nerable golden plumes, is especially common in the dainos. "Here comes the falcon over a green forest." Another song will speak of a green linden as the falcon's home, a stream under the linden as his wine, and dew on the leaves of the linden as his gold.

The widespread, fascinating presence of the falcon or hawk in the Baltic, Slavic, Armenian, and Iranian folklores is rooted in mythology. Why are his plumes golden? Why invulnerable? Is it his acute vision, rapacity, and prowess that have caught the interest of the folksinger? The story of the falcon in folklore goes back to the ancient warrior-god, the god of celestial light, or of constellation, whose Lithuanian name is recorded in the 13th century as Žvorūnas. He has a close relation in Slavic myth-ology: Svarog, who lives on in folklore mainly as Rarog, the super-natural falcon or hawk. Further analogies go back to the Iranian warrior-god Vrthragna, the Indic Indra-Vrtrahan, and the Armen-ian Vahagn. These names are connected with the Lithuanian name for hawk: vanagas. A long list of mythological and linguistic parallels allows the connection of Lithuanian sakalas and vanagas with an ancient mythological divine bird, the incarnation of the warrior-god, the dragon-killer. But the name disappeared from Lithuanian folklore long ago.

Another mythological figure who brings fertility, happiness, and prosperity has deeply absorbed the minds of Lithuanians until very recently: the harmless green snake, called žaltys. It is a blessing to have a žaltys in one's home. He was loved by the sun: "The sight of a dead žaltys makes the sun cry," says a proverb. To kill one is a crime. Žaltys is the messenger of the gods, as an old daina describes him:

> O you žaltys, little žaltys,
> You, the gods' little messenger. . . .

Probably it is safe to conjecture that žaltys is the Baltic equivalent of the primitive Hermes, or phallic herm, of Greek mythology. The Greek Hermes was also god of ghosts and the underworld, the conductor of the souls of the dead to Hades; the Lithuanian žaltys had his palace in the underworld.

The conventional classification of the dainos ascribes to the mythological group only those several songs in which Perkūnas,

21

sun, moon, and stars appear. Yet the old *dainos* are permeated by many more mythological images. The specific attitude toward earth and the living world is inseparable from ancient mythology.

In songs and prayers, Mother Earth has the epithet "moist" (*sieroji žemelė*), as in the ancient Slavic, Greek, and Iranian mythologies. Almost until the 20th century, Lithuanians believed in a personified goddess to whom prayers were said and offerings made. Earth was to be kissed in the morning and evening. Historic records from the 17th-19th centuries mention rhymed prayers to Mother Earth. She is called Žemyna or, in the diminutive, Žemynėlė. She is addressed with picturesque epithets: "bud-raiser," or "blossomer." She guards all earthly life, blesses tillages, forests, fields, leas, pastures, and slopes. All plant life bears witness to Mother Earth's blessings: flowers, green branches, trees "with nine branches." The attitude toward the living world in the *dainos* is not simply lyrical: it is an attitude toward what is sacred. Veneration of sacred forests, trees, and flowers goes back to pre-Christian times, when plant life was enclosed, untouchable, and guarded by tabu.

The green rue, the green branch, the green spruce, linden, or oak are the basic "personages" of the Lithuanian *daina*. They are synonymous with hope and happiness. "The lindens green, green their leaves. . . ." How joyous a statement! Green is the color of the flourishing, verdant earth, a symbol of the farmer's well-being. "Sing, maiden, sing, green is your rue. . . ."

As in folk art, we find in the *dainos* a "cosmic tree," or tree of life:

> A shoot of linden sprouted
> Straight in the plain's green middle.
> A little oriole came flying.
> Beautifully she sang.

This descriptive portrayal carries a symbolic meaning of life forces blossoming with the blessing of the sky—in this case, an oriole.

Three leaves and nine branches are mystical numbers. The linden, spruce, and oak spread into nine branches. But the most sacred part of the tree is the top. It conceals the secret of life, as in a flower-bud or the red "blossom" of a fern—a plant which

22

has no blossoms, but which exists in folk belief as a symbol of happiness, even omniscience.

One *daina* of interest in the group "Love and Courtship" is that which begins: "The oak, the linden, both green and both fair. . . ." The second part of the song speaks of a boy and girl who stand with their hands clasped together. This oneness of human and plant life stems from the belief that the life force, or soul, is the same in man, plant, animal, and bird; and from the belief in metempsychosis. The soul is immortal. At death it goes into a tree—that of a woman, to a linden or spruce; that of a man, to an oak, maple, or birch; or to a bird—cuckoo, dove, falcon, duckling—or sometimes to an animal, even a reptile or insect. A chaste young girl's soul finds its place in a white lily. Souls of ancestors live in the trees or grass of cemeteries, or in fruit trees. A father's soul almost always lingers in an oak, and a mother's in a spruce or linden:

> On Mother's grave
> Grass did not grow,
> Grass did not grow.
> No grass.
> Only a green linden
> Has grown
> With nine branches,
> With a radiant top.

Orphans' songs contain phrases like "green linden, my mother" or "green oak tree, my father."

The life force, Lithuanian *siela*, incarnated in trees, flowers, birds, and animals, is not to be confused with *vėlė*—the shade of a deceased person which continues to live with all its personal characteristics in the realm of death—a hill of *vėlės* where the dead have their houses, tables covered with linen cloths, and benches on which they sit silent and bloodless as Greek *psyches* in Hades. We hear about *vėlės* from the *raudos*, or lamentation songs—extremely simple, touching folk poetry (see under "Laments," page 129). The existence of lamentation songs is witnessed by 13th-century records; they were doubtless sung through many centuries of the prehistoric era.

* * *

23

The antiquity and charming simplicity of the *daina* are not new discoveries. To Lessing, who in 1759 read German translations of three folksongs (translated by Pastor Ruhig in 1745), *dainos* were "precious rarities" which gave him "endless delight." These unpolished, unforced folk creations were to capture the interest and enthusiasm of Lessing and, later, Herder—two poets who began the reaction against pseudo-classicism and a return to simplicity and sincerity. Goethe was also deeply moved by the *daina*. Schumann, Chopin, and Schubert each set to music a poetically translated *daina*. To the Russian poet Balmont, Lithuanian poetry was a "forest fairy." Ludwig Rhesa (1776-1814), the founder of research in the *daina*, said rightly in his introduction to 85 songs with a German translation, published in 1825: "Folk poetry reveals to us a rich treasure, by means of which we may study the human spirit, be it on the shores of Greece or the banks of the Nemunas. A little folksong can show us the customs of a nation more vividly and more sincerely than descriptions of these customs in many volumes." He was the first to speak of the profound antiquity of the *daina* and to publish a number of mythological songs.

Attempts to translate the *daina* must be appreciated, as they involve difficulties that stem from an infinite number of linguistic peculiarities. In spite of such problems, the *daina* has been translated into German, French, Czech, Polish, Russian, Estonian, Finnish, and finally into English. The first ambitious effort to produce English translations was made by Uriah Katzenelenbogen in 1934, in *The Daina, an Anthology of Lithuanian and Latvian Folksongs* (with 98 songs in English and an extensive introduction to the *daina*), more than 100 years after the first German translations had appeared. The translations for *The Green Linden* have been prepared by a group of poets, whose task was to render Lithuanian folksongs as the common poetic heritage of European peoples, in a readable and, if possible, undistorted form. I believe that this volume offers the best translations of the *daina* that have ever been made.

Marija Gimbutas

I. Mythological

The moon wedded the sun

The moon wedded the sun
in the first springtime.

The sun rose in the dawn,
the moon abandoned her,

wandered alone, afar,
and loved the morning star.

Angered, Perkunas thundered
and cleft him with a sword:

—How could you dare to love
the daystar, drift away
in the night alone, and stray?

(Clark Mills)

O little sun, God's daughter

O little sun, God's daughter,
Where have you been dwelling?
Where have you been straying?
Why have you left us alone?

—I have kept shepherds warm,
I have shielded the orphans
Beyond the seas and mountains.

—O little sun, God's daughter,
Who kindled the fires in the evening?
Who kindled the fires in the evening?
Who made your bed for you?

27

—O morning and evening star!
The morning star my fire,
The evening star my bed.
Many kinsmen have blessed me,
And many are my treasures!

(Robert Payne)

Rise, sun

Rise, sun,
Circle the sky,
Make your rounds, counting
To see if the stars
Are all in their places.

I see,
Count or no count,
That one star is missing—
The one that rose first,
Sank last, shone brightest.

(Marjorie Burns)

Fly, hawk, over the lake

Fly, hawk, over the lake.
In that lake a maelstrom spins.

Beside that whirlpool, garden of rue.
In that garden a maiden weeps:

—For me no mother to gather dowry,
for me no father to give my share,

for me no brother, the steeds to saddle,
for me no sister to plait my wreath.

Sun mother, you, sun mother,
sun mother, gather dowry;

moon father, you, moon father,
moon father, give my share;

star sister, you, star sister,
star sister, plait my wreath;

and you, brother Orion,
brother Orion, go with me through the meadow.

(Clark Mills)

Little he-goat, black-bearded

Little he-goat, black-bearded,
Grow up, grow up!
The gods are waiting for thee.
They are waiting.

On the cliff by the river
A fire burns day and night,
Shining like starlight.
    Ruginis, Žvaginis
Will strangle God's little goatling.

During reaping, during sowing
We shall lead thee, little blackbeard,
We shall lead thee to the cliff.
    Ruginis, Žvaginis
Shall strangle thee, little goatling,
    To the glory of God.

(Robert Payne)

I lost my little lamb

I lost my little lamb
Late in the evening.
O, who will help me find
My little lamb?

29

I went to the morning star
And the star answered me:
—I must build a fire
For the morning sun.

I went to the evening star
And the star answered me:
—I must prepare a bed
For the evening sun.

Then I went to the moon
And the moon answered me:
—I have been cut by a sword,
And my face is melancholy.

Then I went to the sun
And the sun answered me:
—Nine days I'll search for you,
And I'll not rest on the tenth.

(Robert Payne)

Three lime trees

Three lime trees in a swamp,
all growing from one stump.

Among these limes by the stream
three maidens wandering came.

The boughs two sisters seized
and in between them squeezed.

But the last was unable to
and fell into the flow.

Her the current carried
towards the Niemen wide.

Her the Niemen did not want
and to the Rusne sent.

Her the Rusne did not want
and to its estuary sent.

Her the estuary would not keep
and back to the shore did sweep.

There into a lime tree green
she grew with branches nine.

Her brother came a flute
to cut from a lime shoot.

—My flute plays beautifully,
its voice speaks mournfully.

But his mother said to him:
—That voice is not from the lime;

that's the soul of my daughter
swimming upon the water.

(Adrian Paterson)

Sister went for water

Sister went for water
With the newest pails
And silken bucket chains.

Cold was the running stream
But not frozen over,
And the plank icy.

And from the glazed plank
She slipped down and down
To the bottom of the earth,
To the land of the sea.

31

There she found her brother
Tending the steeds of God,
Plaiting their silken manes.

—O brother, come home with me.
Mother has waited long,
Our beloved has waited long.

—Dear sister, I cannot yet,
God's horses must I keep,
Yet take this silken scarf:

Wash it with tears, dear one,
Dry it with your sighs,
Calendar it with your elbows, sweet.

She washed it with her tears,
But alas . . .

She dried it with her sighs,
But alas . . .

She calendared it with her elbows,
But alas . . .

She stood a hole into the hill,
But alas . . .

And she outstared the window glass,
But alas . . .

(Remy Limjoco)

O mother sun

O mother sun, to us here, to us here!
O father cloud, to Prussia, to Prussia!
Prussia's hills are alight with flames;
our hills are running with streams,
O mother sun!

O mother, sun, have pity on us here!
O father, cloud, travel to Prussia!
In Prussia's meadows the grass is in flames;
in our meadows all is in streams,
O mother sun!

Blow, wind, blow the cloud from us here to Prussia!
Bear, O wind, the rain from us here to Prussia!
We have had enough of rain!
Oh let there be sun again,
O mother sun!

The cloud travelled to Prussia, to Prussia;
again the sun began to shine for us here, for us here.
O mother sun,
us thou hadst pity on,
O mother sun!

Already clover grows along the fieldway, the fieldway,
and the warm sun gives heat during the day, the day.
O mother sun,
us thou hadst pity on,
O mother sun!

(Adrian Paterson)

Hail to Thee, dear God

Hail to Thee, dear God,
great sower of the sod!

Grant the sheaf yield!
Far my cares drive!
Let the harvest thrive
in the open field!

Oh scatter the seed
through the green mead!
And I beg Thee feed
both ram and steed.

To God in offering
an armful I'll bring.

Sons He does raise
to be my delight,
for my head white
they'll tend in the old days.

A horse too He does rear
my heart to cheer.

(Adrian Paterson)

Side by side

Side by side they sped, two fisherlads
Who would not stay in Rusnes town;
Low, into the Nemunas, they cast
Their slender nets adown, adown.

Raging high, the billow god arose,
Blasting down, the whirlwinds spin.
—O friend, O friend, my own true friend,
Throw the golden anchor in.

—O friend, O friend, my own true friend,
Climb the mast and climb it high.
Say you see the dunes against the hill,
And slender pines against the sky.

I see no dunes, my friend, no slender pines,
No hill, O friend, I tell you true.
I see nothing but a slender girl
Who tends a garden green with rue.

(Demie Jonaitis)

Rise, mother sun

Rise, mother sun, rise!
So small, we shepherds,
and short, our jackets
of fur. We are so cold,
so cold.

(Clark Mills)

A nine-horned stag

A nine-horned stag came running,
Oh, *Kalèda*, a nine-horned stag!
Oh, he came running and looks into the water,
Looks into the water, counting his little horns.
—On my head there are nine little horns,
Nine horns—the tenth, a little branch:
On that branch the little smiths hammer,
The little smiths hammer, the little smiths pour.
Oh, little smiths, my dear brothers,
Forge me a golden cup,
I will sprinkle with water the little green rue.

(Marija Gimbutas)

I walked through the farmyard

I walked through the farmyard
To the high granary,
And I heard a falcon
Singing in the woodland.

—O falcon, little falcon,
You beautiful birdling,
If I could but lure you
Here into my garden,
Then, then, little falcon,
I'd make you drink wine,
I'd strew flakes of gold
On your motley plumage.

35

—No, lad, lure a maiden
Up into your garner;
Not me, a mere birdling,
But a young maiden.
Woodland's green linden,
That's my granary;
Stream under the linden,
That spring's my wine;
Dewdrops on the linden,
They're my flakes of gold.

(Algirdas Landsbergis)

There flew, there flew

There flew, there flew two little gray doves,
Little rue, green rue.
They bore, they bore an oak's little seeds.
On they bore; as they flew, little seeds fell down.
Oh, there grew up two little oaks,
On the little oaks a golden dew.

(Marija Gimbutas)

Morning star lauded her wedding

Morning star lauded her wedding,
but Perkunas rode through the gate,
struck, felled the green oak.

—The oaken blood welled out,
splotched my spotless gown,
spattered my wreath.

Sun's daughter wept
for three years as she gathered
together leaves that had withered.

—Where, O Mother mine,
shall I wash clean the gown?
Where wash the blood away?

36

—Young one, daughter, child,
go to that still pool
where the nine streams flow.

—Where, O Mother mine,
shall I dry out my clothes?
Where in the wind dry them?

—Young one, daughter, child,
in that still garden
where the nine roses bloom.

—When, O Mother mine,
shall I put on the gown?
Walk out in the white gown?

—Young one, daughter, child,
on that miracle day
of nine suns white above.

(*Clark Mills*)

II. Nature

Little tall rye

Little tall rye,
grain son,
shoot that came winning through winter.

In the wide field
you found foothold,
you quickened red

and oh, sprang green
the high hill over,
you gave the field her dear dress.

Deathbound in winter
rye that would-be,
you held out for the bright sun.

Day warm,
night cool,
evening awake,

you grew up stout,
you ripened robust,
to all you are very precious.

Gold ear
of grainlet suns,
tall silver shaftling,

on you
droplets of dew
shine like silver buds.

41

You did not fear
winter cold
nor summer drought.

You feared only
the steel scythe,
the grain son reapers.

(Mary Phelps)

The poplar bloomed

The poplar bloomed, fair on the hill.
O green rye, O beloved.
Tiny, the bees hummed in the valley.
O green rye, O beloved.

(Clark Mills)

Two little bees

Two little bees,
the tiniest bees,
thrummed in the clover.

Collecting what?
Making what?
—Thrummed in the clover.

(Clark Mills)

Equable plains, green meadows

Equable plains, green meadows,
Tiny white clover there commingled.

Within the rich low grass, a brook
Flowed like a string of silver.

A shoot of linden sprouted,
Straight in the plain's green middle.

42

A little oriole came flying.
Beautifully she sang.

And here came three young sisters
For water, for their faces.

(Chi Chou)

The wolf

The wolf, the wolf,
The beast of the forest,
Comes out of the woods
Into the meadow,
Devours the calf
And the little foal:
That is his work.

The fox, the fox,
The beast of the forest,
Creeps out of the woods
And into the yard.
He seizes and kills
The goose and the hen:
That is his work.

The dog, the dog,
Watches the house.
He barks and bites
The heels of the robber.
He scares old women
And wandering people:
That is his work.

The flea, the flea,
The dainty-mouthed beast,
Sucks the sweet blood
At break of day.
He wakes the maiden
To milk the cows:
That is his work.

The bee, the bee,
The dweller of forests,
Hums on the heath,
And stings our fingers
And faces and ears,
And gives us honey:
That is his work.

O man, O man,
Look at the bee—
You sting enough
In the heart, the heart;
Nevertheless, give sweetness
To your own brother:
That is man's work.

(*Uriah Katzenelenbogen*)

Blossom, please blossom

—Blossom, please blossom,
O white apple tree.
Blossom, please blossom,
O dry, leafless one.

—Oh, how can I blossom?
How can a white apple tree
Bear any blossoms
From dry, leafless limbs?

Who will breathe onto me
The green leaves?
Who will heap up on me
The white blossoms?

—The wind—he will breathe onto you
The green leaves.
The sun—she will heap up on you
The white blossoms.

(*Marjorie Burns*)

Comely, the cuckoo sang

Comely, the cuckoo sang
In the grove, combing her hair.

—Look, how fair is my hair!
So much like the summer day.

Fingers covered with rings,
The manor filled with guests.

(Ilona Gražytė and Henrikas Nagys)

It's the rooster's fault

It's the rooster's fault,
The rooster's fault,
He did not love the hen.
In a week, in a week,
She laid only one egg.

(Uriah Katzenelenbogen)

Bruin is running around the reeds

Bruin is running around the reeds,
ruining reeds,
wow, ow, ow-ow-ow,
ruining reeds,

ruining rushes and reeds,
muddling the mud.

Hey, brunette, you gentle cub,
give my little head a rub.

If you press it once or twice,
I shall be in paradise.

The keeper of the inn was here.
That woman—where'd she disappear?

With grain to grind and sacks to fill,
she drove her wagon to the mill.

The while she milled the ripened rye,
she also made her husband die.

The while she bolted meal from bran,
she also lured another man.

(Theodore Melnechuk)

Hoi, you young birdlings

Hoi, you young birdlings,
I wish to be married.
The gray-coated thrush
Will saddle my horses,
The beaver with marten's cap
Will be the driver,
The slender-legged hare
Will be the poursuivant,
The crystal-clear nightingale
Will sing the hymnals,
And the leaping magpie
Will whirl in the dances.

The wolf with his big trumpet
Will play on the pipes,
The bear with huge paws
Will chop up the wood,
The crook-back crow
Will carry the water,
The white-aproned swallow
Will wash all the dishes,
The bushy-tailed squirrel
Will set the table,
And the silk-clothed vixen
Will sit by my bride.

(Robert Payne)

A duckling glides

A duckling glides,
An ash-gray duckling
Over the deep, deep lake.

I'll throw out the net,
A silken red net,
Just like the sunset glow.

I'll pull in the net
And let my children go
And I, I'll fly away.

        (*Ilona Gražytė and Henrikas Nagys*)

Hey, nowhere, nowhere

Hey, nowhere, nowhere,
are there such gardens
as this my father's!
Pearl leaves
and golden flowers
—diamond apples!
Oh, and flying, flying
a speckled cuckoo came
into Father's garden!
And she perched there,
all glitter in the air,
and as she flew away
she tinkled, tinkled.

        (*Clark Mills*)

47

III. Love and Courtship

The oak, the linden

The oak, the linden,
both green and both fair,
stand by the road together.
Branches incline within each other,
leaves interweave in air.

Boy stands, girl stands,
both of them young and fair,
in their clasped hands together.
Their shoulders lean one to the other,
rings of betrothal given.

(Clark Mills)

I had a little brother

I had a little brother,
He was dressed in finery.
He had a brown pony
With golden horseshoes.

When he rode over a meadow,
The meadow trembled.
He cut down the clover
And stamped down the flowers.

When he rode over fields,
The fields roared aloud.
When he rode over the moors,
The moors shouted.

He trod on the prickly thorns
From which the cattle fled.
He met a young maiden,
A white lily.

51

He bade her good morning,
But she did not answer.
He doffed his cap to her,
And she doffed her crown of flowers.

(Robert Payne)

Peony

Peony, so comely,
Kindles as it grows.
Green, my peony is burning,
Red, each blossom glows.

Low I bent the blossoms,
Plucked them from the air,
Wove the glow of blossoms,
Comely, through my hair.

Low the cherry orchard,
Dark the manse above,
Walked I through the cherry orchard,
Chanced to meet my love.

Young is my beloved,
Comely, too, is he,
Cheeks that burn like blossoms
Of the peony.

(Demie Jonaitis)

Ah, sorrow

Ah, sorrow, sorrow,
Ah, my sorrow,
When will you ever cease?

When I grow up
And find my beloved,
Then will my sorrow cease.

(Uriah Katzenelenbogen)

Where is that spring

Where is that spring
Where my young lips drank,
And where is the maiden
I kissed there?

The maiden I kissed
And took to my heart,
And courted each night
In my dreams?

Already that water
Has turned into ice,
And that maiden
Turned to another.

(Marjorie Burns)

I went to the garden

I went to the garden
And I washed my face
With dew from the rue.

I wiped my face
With lily leaves,
With lilies white.

As I bent the lilies
My little ring fell
From my white hand,

And I lost my ring.
Oh, who has seen it?
Return it to me!

It is not my ring:
My lover bought it
As pledge of his love.

(Uriah Katzenelenbogen)

53

Consider, duckling

—Consider, duckling,
As you swim so softly:
Reflect, my little maiden,
If you will marry me.

Little maid, do you know
How to spin, how to weave,
Or how to harvest
The rye on the hill?

—Oh, do not ask
If I know my work,
Just ask, my suitor,
If I'll marry you.

—I am no drunkard
nor a squanderer.
I am my father's son
And a plougher of earth.

Consider, duckling,
As you swim so softly:
Reflect, my little maiden,
If you will marry me.

(Mariejo Fonsale)

Far out on a shoreless ocean

—Far out on a shoreless ocean
I would build a castle,
And you, not quite a woman,
Should be my child-bride.

—Oh, do not lure me yet, lad,
I'm too young for courting.
Leave me safe and carefree
By my mother's side.

54

—It's well for you, my pretty,
Within your mother's gates,
But it's ill for this unlucky fellow
On enemy highways.

Soft beneath your little feet
The meadow will be green,
But under this poor fellow's heels
A blistering fire will blaze.

On your gay, untroubled head
Will rest a wreath of green,
But on my brow a stinging crown
Of blackthorn will be laid.

On your hand a ring will wink
Its spears of golden light,
But in my hand will glitter
A long, blood-letting blade.

About your summer-drowsy head
The honey bees will hum,
While over this forsaken skull
The leaden bullets whine.

A tender mother will your help
And heart's companion be,
But only a violent rifle
Will be a friend of mine.

(Marjorie Burns)

Tall sky, bright stars

Tall sky, bright stars,
Stars big and tiny,
Light the way for me,
Riding to find the girl.

55

—Why come riding, lad,
You unexpected one?
Why sit close beside me,
You I could not love?

Bay steed not yours,
Yet you ride to me.
Ring of gold not yours
You would press on me.

Oh yes, on your brother's
Steed you rode to me.
The gold ring, your sister's,
You would offer me.

(Chi Chou)

Look through the window, Sweet

Look through the window, Sweet.
What winds are there blowing?
—The same wind as yesterday,
The blessed wind from the north.

Give me a ship to sail in
Far over the sea,
And I shall bring home with me
Black silk and green rue.

Black silk for a banneret
Embroidered with fishermen,
And the rue, the green rue
For weaving garlands.

(Robert Payne)

I fed my steed

I fed my steed
All the long summer.
At season's hint I'll saddle him,
My bay steed,
For autumn's journey.

—O my young steed,
O steed,
Will you bear me
Those hundred miles
In one short hour?

—O lad,
O my lad,
Only fill my oat-bag,
Water my thirst,
And I'm yours for the journey.

. . . Another time I rode
By her mother's manor,
To the cherry orchard, green
Where birds warble and twitter.
Oh, how beautiful their song!

(Rita Howes)

Up, to the stone

—Up, to the stone,
Onto the steed,
To pasture we'll ride
To herd the steeds.

We'll herd the steeds,
We'll build us a fire,
The green rue wreath
We'll burn in that fire.

—But the mist is falling,
The dew is falling,
And my maiden's
Bitter tears.

(Remy Limjoco)

Beautiful, the white maiden

Beautiful, the white maiden,
her light a flower's heart!
Apart, her lips that sun me
are honeyed, sweet as plum.

I sicken, dumb with pain;
nor eat again nor drink.
I think: How act, and where,
she from air out of sight?

(*Clark Mills*)

Whiter, whiter, my two white hands

Whiter, whiter, my two white hands I washed.
By the lake I leaned on them; I dreamed.

—Well, you white hands, my two hands,
Who'll get you, who?

A lad, a young, young lad?
Then flax I'll spin—fine, fine, fine.

An old, old man—wife-lost, searching?
Coarse linen I'll weave—heavy, heavy.

(*Rita Howes*)

Under the peonies

Under the peonies,
Under the lilies,
Under the blossoms
The maidens dance.

Oh, if I had the key
To the door of the garden,
I would look,
I could see
A maiden dance.

58

Motley the manor
And the barn so high!
In that high barn must lie
The bed of a maiden.

The bed of a maiden
Softly, softly prepared . . .
Oh, I'd fall into it
And slumber and rejoice!
None would hear my voice.

(Aletta Conway)

Tell me, maiden

—Tell me, maiden,
Tell me, young one,
What grows verdant in the winter
And also in the summer?

—Not a maiden would I be
If I did not know
What grows verdant in the winter
And also in the summer.

In the forest a spruce,
In the flower-garden a rue,
That grows verdant in the winter
And also in the summer.

—Tell me, maiden,
Tell me, young one,
What is lighter
Than a goose feather?

—Not a maiden would I be
If I did not know
What is lighter
Than a goose feather.

My own lad's hands
On my shoulders,
These are lighter
Than a goose feather.

(Algirdas Landsbergis)

Green the linden grows

Green the linden grows
On the green meadow,
On the green meadow.

Under the green linden
Pours forth a river,
Flows the deep water.

My dear mother sent me
There to fetch water,
There to fetch water.

And a morning wind rose,
Blew off my wreath
Into mid-water.

Three youths came riding
To water their horses,
To water their horses.

One has determined
To swim for my wreath,
To swim for my wreath.

If you will reach the bank
I'll be your beloved,
I'll be your beloved.

If you sink to the bottom
You'll rejoice in heaven,
You'll rejoice in heaven.

While the little wreath floated,
The lad sank into the bog,
The lad sank into the bog.

On the bank the wreath lay,
The lad at the bottom,
The lad at the bottom.

In her hands was the wreath,
The lad on the plank,
The lad on the plank.

On the nail her wreath hung,
The lad in his coffin,
The lad in his coffin.

—Do not tell that I
Drowned for the wreath,
Drowned for the wreath.

Only say that I
Watered the roan,
Watered the roan.

Do not bury me
On the high mountain,
Under green lindens.

When you sow the green rue-plants,
Then you will mention me,
Then you will mention me.

When you gather green rue-plants,
Then you will see me,
Then you will see me.

While weaving your wreath,
You will caress me,
You will caress me.

(Uriah Katzenelenbogen)

No one understands

—No one understands
a beautiful riddle,
unless he muses on it.

Rocks are without roots,
water is without wing
and ferns are without flowers.

Even so myself,
a young maiden,
am without a young man.

I shall sell a ring
and a garland
and look for a ploughman.

And a young lad
answerèd
near the green rue bed:

—Sell no ring
and no garland!
I will be a ploughman.

Cold is winter,
cold is autumn,
cold am I, lying alone.

I will sell a horse
and a bridle
and I'll buy a spindle.

And the young maid
answerèd
near the green rue bed:

—Sell no horse
and no bridle!
Hire no spindle!

I will be a spinner,
I will be a weaver,
and a binder of rye.

Finely I'll spin,
closely I'll weave
smocks for a young man.

(Adrian Paterson)

Three youths

Three youths
For me have quarreled.
The first one said:
—The maid is mine.
The second said:
—As the fates decree.
The third I loved,
But he remained
In meditation.

Three maids
For me have quarreled.
The first one said:
—The youth is mine.
The second said:
—As the fates decree.
The third I loved,
But she remained
In meditation.

(Uriah Katzenelenbogen)

Go where green

Go where green, where green,
where green the wood,
where in the wood
a dark tower is hid,

where in the wood
a dark tower is hid,
go where a stripling
sits in that tower.

He does not know yet
of winter cold,
of winter cold,
nor of the summer.

He does not know yet
of daylight breaking,
of daylight breaking,
of the sun's waking.

Oh, cast I would, cast I would
a golden wedge
and send it past, I would,
the window ledge,

and send it past, I would,
the window ledge,
that he may know soon
of daylight breaking,

that he may know soon
of daylight breaking,
of daylight breaking,
of the sun's waking!

Oh, cast I would, cast I would
a ball of snow,
that of cold winter
he may now know!

Oh, cast I would, cast I would
a marjoram broom,
that he may know now
summer is come!

(Adrian Paterson)

I went to the garden

I went to the garden
And I washed my face
With dew from the rue.

I wiped my face
With lily leaves,
With lilies white.

As I bent the lilies
My little ring fell
From my white hand,

And I lost my ring.
Oh, who has seen it?
Return it to me!

It is not my ring:
My lover bought it
As pledge of his love.

(Uriah Katzenelenbogen)

What were you dreaming

What were you dreaming,
O beautiful maid,
To take for your lover
That penniless blade?

A rich man approached me,
Stood close by my side,
His cheeks were like thistle,
Thorny and pied.

My poor love stood distant:
He harrowed below,
His cheeks all aglowing,
Aglowing, aglow.

65

The lands of the rich man
Are wide but untilled;
Scant are my poor love's,
Yet harrowed and filled.

The rich man has oxen
He hires with pelf;
One ox has my poor love,
He reared it himself.

(Demie Jonaitis)

Through the night, the long night

Through the night, the long night,
I scarcely slept a wink.
I went to find my horses
In the green forest.

Morning had not dawned yet,
The sun had not risen
When I heard the latest news
Of my young beloved.

—My dear little maiden,
Have I not warned you
Never to dance with young lads,
Those big stupid boys?

She had plucked the young roses
Whose buds were scarcely opened.
She has flung off the veil
She has scarcely worn.

(Robert Payne)

I was a pilgrim

I was a pilgrim,
And I went on a pilgrimage.
Not far away
I came upon a maiden.

I went beyond the forests,
I went beyond the meadowland.
More than two hundred miles away,
More than three hundred.

The maiden was in flower
In a garden of rue,
Among roses and rue
And the bright carnations.

Tu-whit, tu-whoo!
The maiden in the rue,
How sweet and how lovely
Is my green maiden!

. . . I was a pilgrim
And I went on a pilgrimage.
Not far away
I came upon a boy.

I went beyond the forests,
I went beyond the meadowland.
More than two hundred miles away,
More than three hundred.

The boy was in flower
In a garden of thistles,
Among thistles and burdock,
In the wild nettles.

Tu-whit, tu-whoo!
The boy in the thorns,
How coarse and spiky
Is my thorny boy!

(Robert Payne)

As I went into the lily-garden

As I went into the lily-garden
Five or six fellows stared at me.

As I was leaving the lily-garden,
Five or six raised their hats to me.

As I was dancing with a strange fellow,
They tore my apron with their spurs.

None of them asked whose beloved I was,
But they shoved me into the corner.

And when I danced with my own beloved
They bore me in their arms.

(Uriah Katzenelenbogen)

O thou oak tree

—O thou oak tree,
tree so green,
why this autumn
art not green?

—How this autumn
should I be green?
I heard coming
woodcutters twain.

Many a branch
the first one lopped off
and my summit
the second chopped off.

. . . From this tree's branches
I'll make a bed.
I'll bend a cradling
from this tree's head.

I myself will lay me
on that same bed,
and in the cradling
I'll swing a maid,

half the day through
till breakfast tide.
Oh *chuchia, lulia,*
my very own bride!

(*Adrian Paterson*)

On the edge of Vilnius town

On the edge of Vilnius town
There's a fine rue-garden.
And in it strolled
A pretty maiden
Plucking the green rue.

Many lords came riding,
Courtiers of the king.
They begged, they entreated
With the pretty young maid:
—Pluck us, pluck us green rue.

—No, I'll pick no rue for you,
Nor gather for you flowers.
I, a youthful maiden,
Am a Vilnius patrician,
And unfit for the king's son.

—Oh, I have three carriages
All adorned with gold.
—I, a young girl,
Am a Vilnius patrician,
And unfit for the king's son.

The young patrician was prevailed upon.
She entered in the carriage:
—Oh I, a youthful maiden,
Patrician of Vilnius,
Am fit for the king's son.

69

Through a gate of green copper,
Another of brass,
The third one
Of pure gold,
The young patrician was led.

They drummed on the tambourines,
They thumped on the kettles.
—Now we'll drink wine
From the king's cellar,
In golden beakers.

(Uriah Katzenelenbogen)

A maiden dreamed

A maiden dreamed
Asleep in her bed
That crossing the sea
Her lad had drowned.

—I'd ask my neighbors
Where find my lad?
Haven't you seen
The lad I love?

—We have all seen
The lad you love
Bob on the sea
Like a wanting drake.

—I'd ask my father
Where bury my lad?
Under the altar,
By the church?

I heard them bringing
The lad I love
With marches and organs,
Processions and bells.

A tree is growing
From tears of mine.
May everyone see
How I have loved.

(Theodore Melnechuk)

High on the hill

High on the hill the willows twirled,
High on the hill the willows twirled.
Deep in the dell were waters purling;
Lulling, the waters purled.

There went a maiden walking, bright,
There went a maiden walking, bright.
Bright walked the maiden, lovely lily,
Lovely, a lily white.

Then came a young man riding there,
Then came a young man riding there.
There rode the young man, fair white clover,
Clover so white and fair.

—Maiden, my maiden, young and white,
Maiden, my maiden, young and white,
Where will you sleep, my lovely lily,
Where will you sleep tonight?

—High in my father's barn I'll sleep,
High in my father's barn I'll sleep;
Deep in my mother's bed I'll slumber,
Motley the bed and deep.

(Demie Jonaitis)

Dawn breaks white

Dawn breaks white,
Sunlight bursts upon the dark;
Yet my beloved
Sleeps sweetly on.

My young love sleeps,
And who can wake her?
My bay steed, my own steed
Would be his gift.

My young love sleeps,
And none can wake her.
It has been many dawns
Since last she woke.

(Rita Howes)

IV. Singing and Drinking

Of me, a mere lad

Of me, a mere lad, abroad they spread it
that I could not sing any songs.
If I were to open my musical box
and sing a choice of my songs,
from Tilsit city to Karaliauchus
I should be singing my songs,
and should I not last out singing my songs,
I should take to humming tunes,
and should I not last out humming tunes,
I should take to piping my pipe.

(Adrian Paterson)

Zithers ring

Zithers ring, they clang!
Pipes re-echo, sound!
Daughters-in-law sing,
Echo, cling—unbound!

Riga, street and lane—
berries crown the hill!
Maids of Lithuania
prettily sing their fill.

(Clark Mills)

My singing is done

My singing is done,
My songs are all sung—
Except for just one,
Except for just one.

I'll not sing it now
In this season of snow—
But when the fields thaw,
And I'm at my plow.

Oh, then I'll be singing
My songs made for winning
The hearts of young women
Who weave the white linen.

(Marjorie Burns)

See how clear the beer

See how clear the beer!
Look, here's another pail!
Drink, brothers, yes, drink up,
and I'll help.

Quaff, brothers, drink it up,
and I will help you.
(Once it's time to pay,
I'll take to my heels.)

(Clark Mills)

I drank the beer

I drank the beer,
sweet mead.
Oh, what are these lines
everywhere on my face?

That bitter hop,
the wheat of winter,
is what has written
everywhere on my face.

(Clark Mills)

76

I drank seven

I drank seven,
Nine more to go.
And what happens in my head?
Nothing, nothing, nothing.

I can still climb a footbridge,
Still ride a steed.
What happens in my head?
Nothing, nothing, nothing.

I could go right on drinking,
My thoughts would stay clear,
Ah, but my heart
Would grow so light!

(Rita Howes)

The housewife drank a little sip

The housewife drank a little sip,
out of the little glass a sip
she swallowed, drank and swallowed, yes, she drank!

She drank because she wanted to,
only because she wanted to,
wanted to drink, was glad, yes, glad to drink.

It tasted fine, for none was left,
she smacked her lips and none was left,
nothing was left, nothing, really nothing at all.

That's why she tilted up the glass,
tilted the little glass up high,
tilted it high and rolled it, tilted it up high.

(Clark Mills)

Oho, we, the fellows

Oho, we, the fellows
of Zhemaitia—true Cossacks!*
Sleepless, all our nights;
daylong we carouse.

Daylong we carouse,
at night we lurk, we prowl
in the stuffed warehouses,
grabbing the goods and cash.

The goods we share with the poor,
with the cash we carouse.
The cash means nothing to us
except to carouse.

Run, fellows, into the corners!
Dawnlight's near—it's here!
People are walking about,
peppering us with bullets.

But we drive back the people,
pepper them with our bullets.
The people fall back, scatter—
they hide in every corner!

. . . Ohaie! They've bound our shiny
boots in their iron chains.
They've taken our clothes away,
flung us into their prison.

Our beds white planks, our pastime
pinching the lice away.
Ohaie, ohaie, ohaie, ohaie!
Ohaie, ohaie, ohaie, ohaie!

(Clark Mills)

* Sung of a robber-leader, Raginis, famed for his exploits in the region
of Lithuania known as Zhemaitia. Cossacks, sent to Lithuania to put down
rebellions, were so detested by the people that their name came to mean
"robbers."

Granny had a graybeard goat

Granny had a graybeard goat;
a-hey, da-dum, a graybeard goat.

Old goat fled to fallow fields.

Granny went to seek her goat;
only found his pair of horns.

So, from water, made a malt:
in the one horn, barley grains;
in the other, grains of rye.

Granny brewed delicious beer;
bade the birds to flock around,
but did not invite the owl.

Uninvited, owl still came;
sat where floor met wall and wall.

Sparrow asked the owl to dance;
sparrow stepped in foot of owl.

Sparrow, when owl sued, flew off;
when owl dropped the case, flew back.

(*Theodore Melnechuk*)

V. Marriage

The matchmaker comes

The matchmaker comes—oh, my! oh, my!—
With big wooden shoes. That will be fine!

Big wooden shoes—oh, my! oh, my!—
Fine for the dancing, just fine!

The matchmaker comes—oh, my! oh, my!—
With nose so big. That will be fine!

A big, big nose—oh, my! oh, my!—
Will cover us. That will be fine!

(Ilona Gražytė and Henrikas Nagys)

I've told my mother

I've told my mother, I refused
oh, at least half a summer past!

—Mother, it's time—you should begin,
find you a girl to weave and spin.

I've spun the white flax quite enough,
woven fine linen cloth enough,

hay in the meadow raked my fill,
garnered enough rye on the hill! . . .

O wreath of rue that crowns my head,
how long shall you stay green and glad?

And you, green silken sunlit braids,
how soon, too soon! your luster fades.

And my hair, O my yellow hair,
no longer tousled in the air . . .

I'll visit Mother and not laugh,
unwreathed—but wear my marriage coif.

O marriage coif, my lovely own,
you'll rustle, in the soft wind blown.

And you, my patterns, wound so fine,
in sun will not lose all your sheen.

You, my green silken braids, I'll keep,
and see you on the wall, and weep.

. . . My rings, my golden rings, you must
lie in my dower chest and rust.

(Clark Mills)

Softly, softly

Softly, softly
Run the Niemen's waters;
Still more softly
Talk the little daughters.

—Long I've listened
To our little mother.
—Long I've listened
To our little old one.

—She'll have me marry,
A young lass to an old man.
—She'll have me marry,
A young lass to a young man.

84

—An old man, an old man,
I'll marry him and chide him;
For three days, three days,
In blackest smoke I'll hide him.

For three days, three days,
In smoke he'll meet this daughter.
The fourth day, fourth day,
He'll drink her washing water.

And oh, I shall give him
Work without ease:
To toss this tiny pebble
Beyond the sea of seas.

—A young man, a young man,
With gentle words I'll greet him;
For three days, three days,
With all my love I'll meet him.

For three days, three days
With gentle words I'll greet him;
The fourth day, fourth day,
With good red wine I'll meet him.

And oh, I shall give him
Work soft as loam:
To push this tiny pebble
Down a high hill home.

(*Demie Jonaitis*)

O Mother, my heart and life

O Mother, my heart and life,
Tell me the meaning of my dreams.
A jackdaw flew over the cherry orchard
Spinning green silk
And scattering white pearls.

85

O Son, my heart and life,
I will tell you the meaning of your dreams.
The jackdaw is your bride,
The green silk is her hair,
And the white pearls are tears.

(Robert Payne)

Tell me, my green rue

—Tell me, my green rue,
Have you heard of the north wind,
Have you heard of the hard frost?

They will find you, my green rue,
Your leaves will be torn
And your boughs broken.

—Tell me, child,
Have you heard the shout of the wedding guests
And the proud canter of the bridegroom?

Child,
The wedding guests will come for you
And the bridegroom.
Your face will turn white
And your hands pale.

(Winthrop Palmer)

I am the only daughter

I am the only daughter
Of my loving mother.
There was no task I shirked,
I worked hardily,
Like every girl.

Mother would teach me
How to get up early.
Willingly I rose,
Lighted the fire,
Cooked my mother's breakfast.

86

Mother would teach me
How to spin fine threads.
Dutiful, quick, I spun
And wound the spun threads
Onto thousands of reels.

Mother would show me
How to weave pure linens.
I wove, wrapped and folded,
Rolled the pure linens
Into the crowded coffer.

And now they bear my dowry
Away to a strange land.
Two or three loads of dowry
Pulled by five, six horses—
My family all escort me.

The carts begin to founder,
The cords are torn apart,
They rip and snap apart,
And the heart of a maiden
Wells up with sorrow.

I walk into the store-room,
There the floor trembles,
Trembles under my feet.
My cheeks are wet with tears
As they pour down my face.

(*Chi Chou*)

Whence did it rise

Whence did it rise,
this high hill?
From all my sighs.

Whence flowed this clear
water together?
From tear on tear.

Oh, far away, away
my home lies—
two hundred miles, they say.

Beyond wide seas,
rivers, and forests
of dark trees.

God, pity me,
dear God—this lad,
my true love is not he.

My husband is unkind,
his mother stern,
his sisters of her mind.

With sewing-frame
and my thin needle
I'd swim back whence I came.

Oh, all's forlorn—
needle and frame are broken,
my green silk torn.

I shall go down,
small as a minnow,
and in the seas drown!

Oh, yes, no more
than minnow, I'll
leap up to the shore!

In the wide waters
it's hard, here
where the wave shatters.

(Clark Mills)

Ah rise, bright moon

Ah rise, bright moon,
rise up, you millwheel.
Ah strike, dear God,
strike down my drunkard.

If windy sunset,
cloudbanks redden.

If drunken husband,
eyelids leaden.

(Theodore Melnechuk)

She who wishes to be free

She who wishes to be free
And live in great delight,
Let her marry a forester,

Let her marry a forester.
A wanderer in the woods,
A rover through the nights.

By day in the woods,
By night in the inn drinking—
And no work for her.

(Uriah Katzenelenbogen)

VI. Family Life

Oh the caroling

Oh the caroling of the maidens,
Oh the greenness of their rue;
Sing, maidens, sing,
Green is your rue.

Oh the caroling of the young men,
Oh the whinnying of their steeds;
Sing, young men, sing,
Swift are your steeds.

Oh the caroling of old women,
Oh their carrots growing green;
Sing, old women, sing,
Your carrots are green.

Oh the caroling of the old men,
Oh the greenness of their rye;
Sing, old men, sing,
Green is your rye.

(Demie Jonaitis)

Nowhere

—Nowhere is there quite a lad
like my lad,
my own clover.

Silver-gold, moustache and temples—
there stands my lad,
my own clover.

—Nowhere is there quite a maiden
like my maiden,
my own lily.

Blond her locks, red her cheeks,
a stem her waist,
gentle waist.

—Nowhere is there quite a father
like my father,
my own elder.

Ashen oxen, bay steeds—
here's my father,
my own elder.

—Nowhere is there quite a mother
like my mother,
my own elder.

Silken distaffs, golden spindles—
here's my mother,
my own elder.

—Nowhere is there quite the comrade
like my brother,
my own clover.

Steel scythe, gold his plow—
here's my brother,
my own clover.

—Nowhere is there quite a friend
like my sister,
my own lily.

Rue wreaths, ribbon of silk,
here's my sister,
my own lily.

(Peter Sears)

Oh, the light shines golden

Oh, the light shines golden,
it glistens like a star.
There Mother waits to see me
home from so far, far.

She walks to the end of the manor
and lifts the copper gate.
She asks me, her young daughter,
if I'll stay now, so late.

—Oh, not now, dear Mother,
I cannot stay with you.
I came back looking, Mother,
for my wreath of rue.

. . . O falcon, falcon,
past woods, beyond the heath,
fly to the guileless forests,
bring me back my wreath!

(Clark Mills)

When I was with my mother

When I was with my mother
I worked not in the house,
but instead I railed the garden
in green maple boughs.

Rue I sowèd, mint I sowèd,
I sowèd lily too,
and I sowèd my young days
like the green rue.

Rue burgeonèd, mint burgeonèd,
lily burgeonèd too,
and my young days took on bud
like the green rue.

95

Rue I waterèd, mint I waterèd,
I waterèd lily too,
and I waterèd my young days
like the green rue.

Rue blossomèd, mint blossomèd,
lily blossomèd too,
and my young days took on blossom
like the green rue.

I made rue garlands, I made mint garlands
and lily garlands too.
I made a garland of my young days
like the green rue.

But then there came a village youth
with iron sickle head,
bent on mowing my young days
like the green rue bed.

Rue he scythèd, mint he scythèd,
he scythèd lily too,
and he scythèd my young days
like the green rue.

Rue I raked in, mint I raked in,
I raked in lily too,
and I raked in my young days
like the green rue.

Rue witherèd, mint witherèd,
lily witherèd too,
my young days witherèd away
like the green rue.

Rue they bore off, mint they bore off,
they bore off lily too,
and they bore off my young days
like the green rue.

(Adrian Paterson)

96

Oh, did gold glimmer

Oh, did gold glimmer on the hill,
daulelio, on the hill glimmer?

Ah no, not gold, not silver,
daulelio, no, not silver.

Mother with daughter down the field,
daulelio, walked down the field.

Seemly, the mother taught the daughter,
daulelio, she seemly taught her.

(*Algirdas Landsbergis*)

Far along the meadow

Far along the meadow
Little birches grow;
There are three atossing, toss-toss, tossing,
Whispering together so:

 —If I were a young man,
 A ploughman on the hill,
 All the sorrow, sorrow, oh, the whole world's sorrow,
 With a ploughshare I would till.

 If I were a young man,
 A mounted gallant lord,
 All the darkness, darkness, oh, the whole world's darkness,
 I would lighten with my sword.

Far along the meadow
Little lindens grow;
There are three atossing, toss-toss, tossing,
Whispering together so:

—If I were a maiden,
My mother I would leave;
Of the sorrow, sorrow, oh, the whole world's sorrow,
Finest linens I would weave.

(Demie Jonaitis)

On a bridge I rode

On a bridge I rode
when I fell off my horse;
and I lay in the mud.

And I was left lying there
for three whole weeks.
No one seemed to care.

There neared me in flight
three speckled cuckoos
one dark midnight.

The first cuckooèd
about my feet,
the second about my head,

and the third did start,
of those speckled cuckoos
to sing about my heart.

My beloved at my feet,
at my head my sister,
my mother by my heart.

My beloved shed tears
for three whole weeks,
my sister for three whole years.

Tears my mother shed,
she who nurtured me,
while life was in her head.

My bride along the smooth sward
accompanièd me,
my sister to the churchyard,

but she who nurtured me,
my mother dear,
to our common home country.

(Adrian Paterson)

Late last night

Late last night
I came home.
I found that mother
Had not gone to bed.

By the gleam
Of the splinter-light
Fine linen she
Busily spun.

—Spin thus, mother,
Very finely,
You would marry me
Far from here.

—Spin thus, daughter,
Still more finely,
I will give you in marriage
Far away indeed.

(Uriah Katzenelenbogen)

Beyond my father's gates

Beyond my father's gates
There is a deep, deep lake.

Two ducklings swim about in it,
Quacking as they swim.

99

No, they are not two ducklings.
They are two little brothers.

—Oh listen, little brother,
To the words of our father.

He says he'll buy us horses
And saffron-leather saddles

To carry us far away
Beyond the green forests

Where we shall often weep
And very seldom sing.

No lovely maidens live there.
There are no quiet singing places.

—The lovely maidens live there.
There are quiet singing places.

(Robert Payne)

My dear heart, my mother

My dear heart, my mother,
so little now, so old,
why did you let me be?

Was it for toils, afflictions
and the slanders
of every passerby?

—No, not for afflictions
nor for your toil
nor for the town slanders.

—My dear heart, my mother,
so in your disregard,
why did you let me be?

100

You could have taken me
and thrown me deep,
deep into the lake,

I could have drowned,
become playmate
of all the fishes

that fishermen, amazed,
would lift up in their silken
nets—myself. Strange catch!

Yes! They could have taken
with all their fishes, me
in their webs of silk.

Oh, they could have fished
and easily taken me
in their wide silken nets!

No speckled pike, I could have been
betrothed to a fisherman
and daughter-in-law to fishers.

(Clark Mills)

So the father raised

So the father raised
Nine sons altogether,
And the tenth child came,
A little daughter.

And the oak tree spread
All its nine branches,
And the tenth branch was
At the very top of the tree.

All the nine sons
Were slaughtered in battle,
But the tenth child was
Saved in God's care.

So the father rested
His sorrowful head,
And his heavy heart
Was quiet with grief.

A storm blew down
All the nine branches,
But the very top of the tree
Was kept in God's care,

And the birds flocked to it—
Cuckoo and nightingale,
All sang and lamented
On the very top of the tree.

(Robert Payne)

Husband dear, lying there

Husband dear, lying there soft as silk like a wolf.
I am abandoned like a broken wheel,
I am left alone like a crumbling wall—
Ride on, ride on, bury him deep, let him not return,
Let him not come back to me, let him not slip out
    and ask for parsley.
If the stork comes flying, what will he say?
The cuckoo will come, but he will not mend the fencehole.

(Robert Payne)

VII. Orphans

There is a high mountain

There is a high mountain
Set in the rivers and seas.
On top of the mountain
Rises a green oak tree.

So in despair I swam
And clung to the oak tree.
—Dear oak tree, please change yourself,
Become my father.

And you, dear growing branches
Become arms of flesh-like whiteness,
And you, dear little leaves,
Turn to loving words.

Sorrowing I went away
Weeping bitterly,
For the oak tree has not changed,
Has not become my father.

And the dear growing branches
Are no arms of flesh-like whiteness,
And the little green leaves
Have not turned to loving words.

(Robert Payne)

The woods are green

The woods are green, green their lindens.
Green the lindens, green their leaves.

I, orphaned and without a father,
am a pied ox with no ploughman.
The woods are green, green their lindens.

105

I, orphaned and without a mother,
am naked distaff with no spinner.
The lindens green, green their leaves.

I, orphaned and without a brother,
a sharpened scythe with no mower.
The woods are green, green their lindens.

I, orphaned and without a sister,
finest of linen with no weaver.
The lindens green, green their leaves.

(*Clark Mills*)

Oh, I was bidden

Oh, I was bidden, bidden
by my stepmother go
for winter green stuff
and summer snow.

And weeping sadly,
as I walked in vain,
I chanced on a youth,
a shepherd swain.

—And whither wilt thou,
my little maiden,
and wherefore weepest,
my little maiden?

—Oh, I'm bidden, bidden
by my stepmother go
for winter green stuff
and summer snow.

—Go, little maiden,
go, young one, go
where the wood borders
on the sea's flow.

There thou wilt come on
a green yew. Take home
boughs of that yew tree
and a handful of sea foam.

For thy stepmother
thou'lt have fetched so
winter green stuff
and summer snow.

(Adrian Paterson)

Flames are blazing beyond the lakes

Flames are blazing beyond the lakes.
I am blinded by my tears.

From the fires, sparks are falling.
So are tears, from me, a girl.

The woods are sad without their cuckoo.
Sad as me, with no more mother.

Dreary, not to have their woodpecker.
Dreary, having no more father.

(*Theodore Melnechuk*)

O earth, my earth

O earth, my earth,
Earth ashen-gray.
You took my father,
Mother away.

You took my father,
Mother away.
So come for me too,
Me, maid and gay.

(*Ilona Gražytė* and *Henrikas Nagys*)

By the white toppling sea

By the white toppling sea,
by blue plunging water,
oh there, there rose
a deep green sycamore.

Under the sycamore,
the hundred-shouldered,
oh there, there stood
the two young sisters.

Shawled in the foam
their salt tears washed,
one spun for the other
a deep-water thought.

—With what shall we wash
our young white faces,
with what shall me comb
our sun-spun braids?

—With the foam we breathe
shall we wash our faces,
with a deep-water perch,
spin our toppling hair.

(Peter Sears)

Ah groaning, groaning

Ah groaning, groaning
was the North Wind!
Ah moaning, moaning
a young village hind!

Then ceased from groaning
the North Wind;
then ceased moaning
the young village hind.

108

O sorrow, sorrow,
sorrow mine, I pray
I may soon sorrow
you utterly away!

Yet when I did pass
along the highway,
there my sorrow was
in mid roadway.

Five score brothers thundered
on down the street,
trampling with four hundred
war horses' feet.

Oh then I implored
that brotherhood
my sorrow to tread
hard under foot.

I begged them to crush it,
my sorrow, with their might;
I asked them to slash it
with their swords bright.

Crushing, they crushed it;
with swords they slashed it;
but my sorrow cared not
that they had lashed it,

but my sorrow cared not,
paid that no heed.
Its trunk swoll instead
and leaves burgeonèd.

Its leaves burgeonèd
and its branches spread,
for my sorrow cared not,
paid that no heed.

When of my mother
I go the way,
then I shall sorrow
my sorrow away.

My darling mother
on the hilltop high,
on the hilltop high
in new grave does lie.

I shall only sorrow
my sorrow away
when of my dear mother
I go the way.

(Adrian Paterson)

VIII. Work

Valio, *scythe!*

Valio, scythe! Friend
to mow the hay.
Unwhetted, you will
down no hay.

Scythe I pulled,
for evening waited.
Hard, that long pull,
hard the long wait.

Valio, how rings
the silver scythe!
Stung by high sun,
copper handle flashes.

At home in my hand,
the new scythe handle!
The lord's meadows
foreign to my feet.

Cranes cross green fields
in slow stilt walk.
We, the young fellows,
trudge his green meadows.

The sun slips down
past the green forest.
The dew silvers
the green grass.

Sun falls west, and maiden
lies in her featherbed.
We, the young fellows,
mowing the hay.

(Peter Sears)

Through the fields lowing

Through the fields lowing, the oxen are coming home
and we walk with them, sisters joyfully singing.

Hola, come out, our brother ploughman, come!
Hola, open the wide green copper gate!

Hola, open the wide green copper gate!
Your ash-colored oxen are here to be let in.

Hola, let in your ash-colored oxen, please,
and let her sleep, your maiden who tends the oxen.

(Clark Mills)

The day is darkening

The day is darkening,
The light is darkening
Into dusk, into dusk.

Ah, the sun is sinking
Into dark clouds
Beyond green forests.

Tomorrow the sun will rise
Into misty clouds
Above green forests.

It will make a bright shimmering
As the mist falls,
As the warm rain falls.

Sisters, let us reap,
Let us hurry, girl-reapers,
Let us pile the shocks.

114

Let us pile the shocks
As snug as we can,
Let us bind the sheaves.

Let us bind the sheaves,
The biggest ones,
Let us finish the rye.

Let us finish the rye,
The ripest stalks,
The ripest stalks.

(Marjorie Burns)

There had come

There had come, there had come,
there had come here
from the town of Gilija
a ship of juniper.

Then my old father
I asked to tell
where the ship to steer,
where to set sail.

Should it be for the deep
or for the shallows?
Neither for the deep
nor for the shallows!

But for an open port
where dwells a maid
in a lofty cottage,
her trim homestead.

There the fair maid stays,
daughter of the days,
weaving and ravelling
and embroidering

from the very corners
in circles of thread
many a red
and green flower head,

and in the middle,
right in the middle,
a yellow sun
with the stars little.

(Adrian Paterson)

Olia, *bossy*

Olia, bossy, moo-cow madcap, bossy my rascal,
Olia, moo-cow, mud-wader, milk-maker,
Olia, bossy, silverhoof, goldhorn,
Come back here, come near me, come mooing!
Come bending the berry-bush, mashing the mire mound, wading
the puddles,
Olia, come mooing, come hunting your herd!
Olia, come running, bossy, come trotting,
parting the underbrush, counting the places, sniffing the steps!
Olia, bossy, come running at the sound of the trees,
at the sound of my voice!
Here's your herd here, come wandering this way.
Here's a place peaceful, green grassy and clovered!
Olia, bossy, my little one,
Olia, bossy, through the dawn's dewdrops,
through the green grassblades, through the white cloverbuds,
eat sweetly, eat neatly!
Olia, eat up, eat up, through meadow and meadow,
with milk fill a pail apiece, pail apiece!

Edro, old ox, my plow-puller, breadbringer!
Edro, old far-furrow, yoke-choker ox!
Edro, old ox, my puller of plowshares.
Edro, my work ox, come along with me lowing,
here's a soft spot and your cow companion!
Olia, olia, olia!

(Theodore Melnechuk)

116

Roar, roar, my millstones

Roar, roar, my millstones!
They think I do not grind alone.

I ground alone, I sang alone,
alone I turned the stone.

—Dear lad, why did you press me,
me, maiden of such woes?

Heart's lad, didn't you know
I wasn't in the manor house, at ease?

Into the marsh up to my knees,
into the water to my shoulders . . .
My days are hard!

(Clark Mills)

The lord of the manor

The lord of the manor
comes devil-faced,
his steward moves
like a thunderclap.

I'd grind that lord
to a fine powder,
crumple his steward
and pound him, mash him.

Their bones would sift
down through a sieve,
and a storm would wash
their bones away.

(Clark Mills)

IX. War

We were five brothers

We were five brothers
On the green meadow.
The next day we were
The crusaders' spoil.

And when they seized us
Five youthful brothers,
They fettered our feet
In chains of iron.

Our feet were fettered
In chains of iron.
They drove us on foot
As far as Tilsit.

The crusaders' chief
Immeasurably cruel
Ordered green willow
To be brought to him.

And when presently
The green willow was brought
He placed us in twos
Apart from the rest.

Then when they beat us
The blood began flowing
Down to the earth,
The earth began shaking.

By the road remained
A streamlet of blood;
And bitter tears
Also were flowing.

The blood on the ground
Began to flower;
And all the kings there
Were looking upon it.

—O mighty rulers,
Grant us a favor;
What do you demand
After such service?

When the sparks fly up
From the hard steel,
Soon none remain
Where they have been.

—O mother, mother,
Why do I still live?
Would that you sooner
Had drowned your son!

—Thank you, dear mother,
For your kindness;
Thank you, dear father,
For your white bread!

—You saw, my parents,
The birth of your son.
But may you not see
His doom approaching.

And on the streets,
Is constant shouting:
—Protect your dear son's
Dead body!

Unburied,
It lies on the ground,
Where dogs are tearing
The feet and the hands.

(Uriah Katzenelenbogen)

Hey, they drove, drove

Hey, they drove, drove,
The village chieftains drove
Us, three young brothers.

Three young brothers, young!
Driven onward and on
Into a foreign land.

Hurled beyond Berlin
Two hundred miles away.
We lay in a tired camp.

Rain fell,
Snow fell,
Ice fell down on us.

Our shoes rotted away
And the socks on our feet,
Our tunics from our shoulders.

I went back home.
No father there for greeting
Nor my old mother.

I went into the orchard.
The ancient oak was gone,
No sign of the green linden.

(*Chi Chou*)

Nobles of Lithuania

Nobles of Lithuania saddled up their steeds,
saddled their steeds to ride away to war.

The first sister polished the brothers' swords,
the second helped them don their battle dress.

123

And the third sister, she who was the youngest,
opened the gate wide and wept for sorrow.

—O brother, brother of mine, my own brother,
can you still overtake the troop of riders,
and find the enemy host, and hew and slash?

—Yes, I shall overtake and I will slash,
but God alone knows if I shall return.

—My sisters, let us go to the broad highway,
it may be we shall live to see our brothers.

On a hill we stood, and our feet dug a pit,
we leaned, and wore an ash-tree fence away.

. . . But did not live to welcome our own brother,
brother of ours, the dearest and the youngest.

His steed ran back alone, whinnying loud,
at his side the stirrups free as pendulums.

—You steed, O dark bay steed, tell us, tell us,
where did you leave our own, our dearest brother?

—If I must tell you, you will weep for sorrow,
and if I do not, all the grief is mine.

Your brother rests in Riga town today,
he rests in Riga town, in a strange land.

I plunged into nine rivers, swam across,
into a tenth I plunged, and plunged across.

Nine bullets, nine! hissed and slapped past,
and the tenth bullet found your youngest brother.

Where his head lay still on the still earth,
a bush of roses flowered, beautiful.

And as the droplets of his fierce blood scattered,
beautiful, the red jewels gleamed and glistened.

(Clark Mills)

O cherry, cherry

—O cherry, cherry,
cherry tree dear,
why dost not blossom
in winter, in winter?

—Frost freezes my blossom,
my blossom, my blossom,
wind cracks my branches,
my green branches.

—O brother, brother,
my brother dear,
why dost not gallop,
being young to the war?

—O sister, sister,
my sister dear,
sister, thou knowest not
how cruel is war.

There stand regiments,
many a regiment,
like the black cloud banks
in the firmament.

There swords, many a sword,
many a sword glitters
as in the high firmament
the brightest stars.

There bullets, bullets,
many a bullet flies,
as in Father's garden
the bees, the bees.

(Adrian Paterson)

Where are you going, my young fellow?

Where are you going, my young fellow?
—To Paris hundreds of miles away, my dear maiden.
What will you wear there, my young fellow?
—A uniform of green silk, my dear maiden.
Where will you stay there, my young fellow?
—By the great River Marne, my dear maiden.
Where will the trumpets blow, my young fellow?
—On the high hill, Montmartre, my dear maiden.
Where will you rest there, my young fellow?
—In the thick of battle, my dear maiden.
Who will sing your praises, my young fellow?
—Muskets and trumpets, my dear maiden.
Who will carry you, my young fellow?
—Courtiers, young generals, my dear maiden.
Where will they bury you, my young fellow?
—Under the church tower, my dear maiden.
Shall we toll the bells, my young fellow?
—Both bells, both together, my dear maiden.
Shall we light the candles, my young fellow?
—A hundred candles together, my dear maiden.

(Uriah Katzenelenbogen)

The son of Kosciuszko

The son of Kosciuszko lies on the battlefield,
For his death was deserved, being obstinate—
Wilfulness was his undoing, nor would he listen
To father or mother, or anyone at all
Of his own standing.

126

So let a letter be written: let it be written quickly,
And let his father make quick reply,
So that we may know where to bury him.
High in the mountain under an oak tree,
In the white sands.

There in the white sands under the oak tree
The green oak shall become his father,
And the white sands will become his mother,
And the green maples will be his brothers,
And the lindens his sisters.

(Robert Payne)

Sing, my dear sister!

Sing, my dear sister! Tell me why you do not sing.
And why lean on your hands, that are so tired already?

—How can I sing? And how could I be gay and joyous?
Disaster walks my flower-garden, yes, disaster.

The rue is trampled and the roses crushed and culled,
the lilies scattered and the dew-drops brushed away.

—But did the north wind blow? Or the river overflow?
Or did the thunder burst and lightning strike from heaven?

—The north wind did not blow, nor the river overflow,
nor thunder burst, nor lightning flash down out of heaven.

No, bearded men, men who invaded from the seas,
climbed up the shore, despoiled the garden of my flowers.

They trod over the rue, they crushed and culled the roses,
scattered the lilies and the dew-drops brushed away.

And even I scarcely endured, by miracle,
beneath a spray of rue—beneath an ebon wreath.

(Clark Mills)

We shall drink beer today

We shall drink beer today.
Tomorrow we'll set forth
for the Magyar land.

There, rivers are wine
and apples, golden—
the forests, orchards.

And what shall we do
in the Magyar land?

There we'll build us a city
with precious jewels
and window-sunlets.

And when shall we return
from the Magyar land?

When pikestaffs burst with buds
and stones explode with flowers
and trees grow on the sea.

(Clark Mills.

X. Laments

They hired me to mourn for you

They hired me to mourn for you,
And weep in lamentation.
They promised me a sieve of beans,
And a bountiful supply of lard.

I wonder: will they pay me or not?
Should I mourn or not?
Should I lament or not?

Help me out, sister,
Where have you hidden your wool?

Little sister, I have found
A song of lamentation.
Deep in my heart I found it.
Just yesterday you baked white loaves
—Now you are lying on a plank.

(Uriah Katzenelenbogen)

Oh, my dear child, my son,

Oh, my dear child, my son, oh, what has frightened you? Was it the hard years, or my hard labors, or my hard life? You would not have been afraid—beside your father, your mother.

Oh, my dear child, my earth's blossom, my forest-nestling, my heaven's star, my mountain-berry!

Oh, my dear child, oh, I imagined, oh, I thought there was no place for my son! Oh, still there were hollows, still there were dales, there was a place for my dear child.

Oh, my father, my mother, oh, I am letting my child go who understands nothing, oh, who knows nothing yet! Oh, my father, oh, my mother, oh, take him by his white hands, seat him on the bench of the shades—oh, teach my child!

(Algirdas Landsbergis)

Sister, my lily, my carnation

Sister, my lily, my carnation, sister, how can we ever part? Wherever, when we met, we chattered our hearts' fill; now you abandon me.

Now with the feast-day coming, the great fair, sisters of everyone will gather, meet in bands, they'll chatter their hearts' fill. Whom shall I choose for sister, as my friend—the speckled cuckoo?

Oh, we two flew to meet together, chattered together like two cuckoos perched beside a fence.

O Father, O my Mother, you have such a large band in the other world; you've sons and daughters, sons-in-law as well.

And we were sisters like two speckled cuckoos—these you tore apart, and it was she you took away from me.

(*Algirdas Landsbergis*)

My Mother, I shall bow

My Mother, I shall bow down to your feet that bore me, and to your hands that lifted me—down to your mouth that spoke to me and taught me chores.

Oh, none has taught the things you knew; you finished all the chores; you raised us all, consoled us all; oh, held us all close.

You left an orphan like a duckling in a pond; I wade through cares as if through mire, through tears as if through water; hard, the bench of orphans; I sat on the plank and the plank gave way.

Oh, I'd go to the green woodland, yes, I'd stand under the green birch; the branches of the birch feel no love, the branches of the birch give pain, pain!

132

Dear Mother, silent, proud, I speak so much to you, I talk to you too much! Ah, why do you not speak a word? Your heart has changed into a pebble—once you spoke, once you loved enough; oh, I'd beg the cuckoo of the woods for spells to make you speak!

Grandfathers—weak my mother's strength, small her forces; lift up the gate of souls, open the door of the souls wide; take her, lead her by her small white hands, bring her to rest upon the narrow bench of souls.

Dear Mother, little is your strength, your power small; long your voyage, dark your abode, dark the lodging without door or windowpane.

(*Algirdas Landsbergis*)

Selected Bibliography

Primary Sources

Balys, Jonas, *Lietuvių dainos Amerikoje*. Lithuanian folksongs in America; narrative folksongs and ballads. Lietuvių enciklopedijos leidykla, Boston, 1958. Texts of 472 songs, with 250 melodies. Foreword and summaries of songs in English.

Čiurlionytė, Jadvyga, *Lietuvių liaudies dainos*. Lithuanian folksongs. Valstybinė grožinės literatūros leidykla, Vilnius, 1955. Texts in Lithuanian and Russian of 295 songs, with melodies and musical explanations.

Jonynas, A., *Dainos. Lietuviu tautosaka*. Songs. Lithuanian folklore. Vol. 1. Valstybinė Politinės ir Mokslinės Literatūros leidykla, Vilnius, 1962.

Juška, Antanas, *Lietuviškos dainos*. Lithuanian folksongs. Valstybinė grožinės literatūros leidykla, Vilnius, 1954. Three vols. Photographic reproduction of 1st ed. (1880-1882), with modern page-by-page transcription. Contains 1,569 songs, with music.

Juška, Antanas, *Lietuviškos svotbinės dainos*. Lithuanian wedding songs. Valstybinė grožinės literatūros leidykla, Vilnius, 1955. Two vols. Texts of 1,100 songs. First ed. of texts published in Petersburg, 1883, and with melodies, in Krakow, 1900. Includes descriptive notes on wedding customs.

Krivickienė, Gražina, *Dainos: vieux chants lithuanians*. Edwin Burda, Fribourg en Brisgau, 1948. Contains 90 folksongs from Liudvinavas and vicinity. With essays by Jonas Balys and Aleksis Rannit and illustrations by Viktoras Petravičius.

Nesselmann, Georg H. F. (tr.), *Dainos. Littauische Volkslieder*. Lithuanian folksongs. F. Dümmler, Berlin, 1853. Contains 410 songs in Lithuanian and German, with 53 melodies.

Rhesa, Ludwig J. (ed. and tr.), *Dainos oder litthauische Volks-lieder. Dainos*, or Lithuanian folksongs. New ed., Vilnius, 1958. First ed., Königsberg, 1825.

Slaviūnas, Zenonas, *Sutartinės: daugiabalsės lietuvių liaudies dainos.* Polyphonic Lithuanian folksongs. Valstybinė grožinės literatūros leidykla, Vilnius, 1958-1959. Three vols., with music.

Translations

Engert, Horst (tr.), *Aus litauischer Dichtung*. Folksongs, poetry, sayings, and miscellanea, in German translation. Pribačis, Kaunas-Leipzig, 1938.

Gregor, Josef (ed.), *Europäische Lieder in den Ursprachen*. European songs in their original languages. Verlag Merseburg, Berlin, 1960. Includes eight Lithuanian songs, with German translations and music.

Katzenelenbogen, Uriah, *The Daina*. An anthology of Lithuanian and Latvian folksongs. Lithuanian News Pub. Co., Chicago, 1935.

Landsbergis, Algirdas, and Mills, Clark, *The Green Oak: Selected Lithuanian Poetry*. Voyages Press, New York, 1962.

Morici, Giuseppe (tr.), *Canti populari Lituani*. Lithuanian folksongs. Second ed., Rome, 1930. Italian prose versions of 303 dainos.

Paterson, Adrian (tr.), *Old Lithuanian Songs*. Introduction by Martin Lings. Pribačis, Kaunas, 1939.

General

Balmont, Constantin, "La Lithuanie et la chanson." Translated from the unpublished Russian text by O. V. de L. Milosz. *Mercure de France*, vol. 211, 1929.

Balys, Jonas, *Lithuania and Lithuanians: a Selected Bibliography*. Frederick A. Praeger, New York, 1961.

Balys, Jonas, *Lithuanian Narrative Folksongs*. A description of types and a bibliography. Draugas Press, Washington, D. C., 1954.

Gimbutas, Marija, *The Balts*. A complete survey of Baltic culture from the 2nd millennium B.C. to the 13th century A.D. Frederick A. Praeger, New York, 1963.

Lituanus (renamed *The Lithuanian Review* in 1964), P.O. Box 9318, Chicago 90, Illinois. A quarterly, 1954—. Contains articles and studies on all aspects of Lithuanian history and culture, including folklore.

Maceina, Antanas, *Das Volkslied als Ausdruck der Volksseele; Geist und Charakter der litauischen Dainos*. Baltisches Forschungs-Institut, Bonn, 1955.

Mauclère, Jean, *Contes lithuaniens: essai de folklore*. F. Lanore, Paris, 1945.

Milosz, O. V. de L., *Oeuvres complètes*, vol. 5: *Contes et fabliaux de la vieille Lithuanie*; vol. 6: *Contes lithuaniens de ma Mère l'Oye, Origines de la nation lithuanienne, Dainos*. Editions Egloff, Paris, 1944-1948.

Senn, Alfred, *The Lithuanian Language: a Characterization*. Lithuanian Cultural Institute, Chicago, 1942.

Vaičulaitis, Antanas, *Outline History of Lithuanian Literature*. Lithuanian Cultural Institute, Chicago, 1942.

Zobarskas, Stepas, *Selected Lithuanian Short Stories*. Preface by Charles Angoff, introduction by Clark Mills. Manyland Books, 1963.

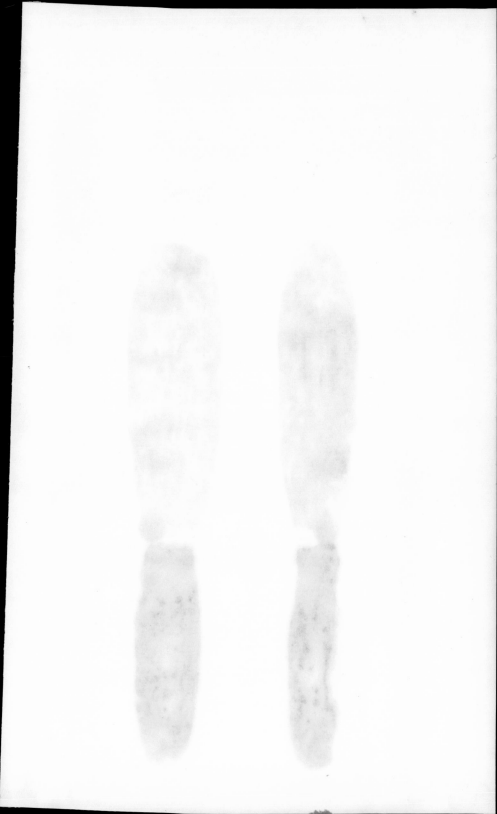

DATE DUE
